THE LIBRARY OF AMERICAN LIVES AND TIMES™

GEORGE WASHINGTON CARVER

The Life of the Great American Agriculturist

Linda McMurry Edwards
Professor Emeritus
North Carolina State University

The Rosen Publishing Group's
PowerPlus Books™
New York

*To my daughter, Parie Hines, who has combined
her many talents to make the world a better place,
just as George Washington Carver did.*

Published in 2004 by The Rosen Publishing Group, Inc.
29 East 21st Street, New York, NY 10010

First Edition

*Editor's Note: All quotations have been reproduced as they appeared in
the letters and diaries from which they were borrowed. No correction was
made to the inconsistent spelling that was common in that time period.*

Library of Congress Cataloging-in-Publication Data

Edwards, Linda McMurry.
George Washington Carver : the life of the great American agriculturist /
Linda McMurry Edwards.
   v. cm. — (The library of American lives and times)
Includes bibliographical references (p.   ).
Contents: The peanut man—Growing up in Missouri—Seeking an
education—In college at last—To be of the greatest good—A challenging
task—The Experiment Station and teaching farmers—Carver's message
for the South—The Wizard of Tuskegee—Carver's final years and legacy.
  ISBN 0-8239-6633-X (lib. bdg.)
1. Carver, George Washington, 1864?–1943—Juvenile literature. 2.
African American agriculturists—Biography—Juvenile literature. 3.
Agriculturists—United States—Biography—Juvenile literature. [1.
Carver, George Washington, 1864?–1943. 2. Agriculturists. 3. Scientists.
4. African Americans—Biography.] I. Title. II. Series.
  S417.C3 E37 2004
  630'.92—dc21

                                     2002151881
                                     Rev.

Manufactured in the United States of America

CONTENTS

1. The Peanut Man

In 1921, members of the U.S. Congress were surprised to see a clean but shabbily dressed black man stand before them as an expert witness. The congressmen were seeking advice about putting a tax, known as a tariff, on peanuts grown outside of the United States. Before 1920, few American farmers planted peanuts, and most Americans bought peanuts that had been grown in other countries. When American farmers began planting peanuts, there were so many foreign peanuts that the farmers could not get good prices for their crops.

A group of peanut farmers knew that George Washington Carver had developed numerous uses for peanuts. They asked Carver to testify in support of a tariff on foreign-grown peanuts. If the foreign peanuts were taxed, the peanuts grown by American farmers would be lower priced in comparison and would have a better chance of being sold to American consumers.

Opposite: This hand-colored photo of George Washington Carver was taken around 1915. In the lapel of his jacket Carver usually wore a fresh flower, a piece of evergreen, or a few berries attached to a twig. The flowers and the greenery were to remind him of God's creations.

This meeting occurred at a time when people were more likely to ridicule African Americans than to listen to them. Indeed, when George Washington Carver began to talk, some members treated him as if he were an amusing joke and laughed at him. They ignored the fact that Carver was a graduate of the nation's leading agricultural college who had spent twenty-five years as an agricultural researcher and teacher. To them he looked more like a janitor than a professor. Before long, however, Carver had won their respect with both his humor and his knowledge of peanuts and agriculture. Someone later said that Carver "soon had them each and every one leaning over the railing to see what was coming next and to get every word spoken."

After that day, Carver was called the Peanut Man. Farmers who grew peanuts came to him for advice. Everyone was amazed by the hundreds of products he made from peanuts, including milk and coffee. Although Carver became famous for his inventions from peanuts, he was much more than a peanut magician. From 1896 until his death in 1943, he worked to improve the lives of poor farmers in Alabama and the rest of the South.

Most farmers in the South did not own property and had to work on other people's land. Some of them did all the work on a farm for a share of the crops. They were called sharecroppers. The landowners usually got about half of the crops from the sharecroppers who farmed the land. From the time they planted the seeds until the time they harvested crops, sharecroppers didn't make any money. To buy food and clothes before the harvest, the sharecroppers had to borrow money from the landowners or bankers and buy their goods on credit, promising to pay the debt at a later date. Generally, the sharecroppers had to pay higher prices for these goods, as well as interest, a fee for the use of the money. Often sharecroppers did not make enough money from the harvest to pay back all that they had borrowed. Debtor laws in many southern states forced them to work for a landowner until they had paid back the money owed. Many black and white sharecroppers became trapped by debt and were forced to work in conditions that resembled slavery. For their labor, many sharecroppers earned only a few pieces of clothing, bad food, and a house without windows or floors.

When Carver arrived in Alabama in 1896 to teach at the Tuskegee Normal and Industrial Institute, he realized that sharecroppers needed to reduce their expenses and to increase their harvests in order to escape from debt. Farmers who sharecropped were too poor to afford the fertilizer and machinery that more successful farmers used. Carver therefore tried to find ways that the sharecroppers could use what they found in nature to replace items that cost money. By showing farmers how to make things for themselves from natural resources, Carver helped many sharecroppers to pay off what they owed. Some sharecroppers even bought their own land, where

This 1881 photograph shows the original site of Tuskegee. The following year the college purchased 100 acres (40.5 ha) of farmland. This property would house the Tuskegee Normal and Industrial Institute campus in Tuskegee, Alabama.

they could keep all that they grew and could make better lives for their families.

Just as sharecroppers depended too much on purchased goods, the South was too dependent on one crop, cotton. Before the Civil War, people all over the world wanted cotton products. Farmers could make money more quickly by planting cotton than by planting any other crop. Southerners said, "Cotton is king," and the South became wealthy. However, cotton plants used up the nutrients in the soil, making it less and less able to grow cotton crops in successive years. After the Civil War, the region became poorer than the rest of the nation. Carver realized that farmers needed to diversify, or start planting other crops. He encouraged them to do so by finding ways to make other crops as desirable as cotton.

Carver could educate sharecroppers and the rest of the South because of his vast knowledge of nature. He understood how plants and animals depended upon each other, and how both plants and animals relied on minerals and the weather. Carver saw a balance and harmony in nature. He understood that people could destroy this balance. Every action they took had an impact on the environment. Thus Carver became a pioneer in teaching people how to use nature safely and therefore to conserve it for future generations.

Carver also believed that there should be harmony between people. However, he lived in a time when many white people thought that people with darker skin were inferior. Most African Americans had been slaves before 1865, and many whites sought to keep the recently emancipated slaves poor and powerless. Segregation laws required black southerners to sit in separate places from whites and to go to different schools, libraries, restaurants, and hospitals. These separate places were usually not nearly as nice as the places for white people. Black southerners who did not follow these rules might be attacked or even killed by angry whites. In those troubled times, Carver became one of the few African Americans to earn the respect of both blacks and whites. They admired his abilities and hard work. His rise from slave to professor impressed them. Carver used his influence to help lessen the hatred toward darker skinned people.

Although Carver was a scientist, an inventor, and a scholar, he should perhaps be best remembered for his teaching. The students in his classrooms loved him and wanted to do their best for him. However, Carver's teaching was not limited to classrooms. He took a "movable school" out to where farmers were working in the fields. Carver gave speeches to groups of white and

This early-twentieth-century sign shows an example of segregation. African Americans were directed to use a separate back entrance. Segregation laws were created after the Civil War to keep the social divisions between blacks and whites in place.

black college students as well as to farmers' groups. Booker T. Washington, the president of Tuskegee Institute and Carver's boss, recognized Carver's talents, saying, "You are a great teacher, a great lecturer, a great inspirer of young men and old men." Overcoming the obstacles of slavery and poverty, Carver used those talents to make a difference.

2. Growing Up in Missouri

George Washington Carver was born in Diamond Grove, Missouri, during the Civil War. As were many children born into slavery, George was unsure of his birthday. The date of his birth was probably in 1864 or 1865. The people in the North and the South were fighting, mainly over the issue of slavery. The Civil War was a bloody war that tore apart families and killed more than 600,000 Americans. Most states that allowed slavery joined the Confederate States of America, but Missouri was a slave state that remained in the Union. Many Missourians, however, believed that the state should fight on the side of the Confederacy. Therefore neighbors often became enemies and fought one another, both on the battlefields and in the streets. Taking advantage of the confusion, outlaws roamed the state in gangs. Some robbed

Opposite: Diamond Grove, Missouri, has been circled in blue in this 1872 Missouri railroad map that was created by Asher & Adams.

MISSOURI

ASHER & ADAMS'
MISSOURI.

Moses Carver, George's foster father, was known by his neighbors as an independent, quiet farmer who loved animals. Moses had a pet rooster that perched on his shoulder. In addition to keeping livestock, Moses employed his skill with creatures as a beekeeper and a race-horse trainer and would later sell the horses that he had trained.

people; others frightened those who did not support their side in the battle.

The war had a great impact on everyone, and George was no exception. The war cost him his mother and won him his freedom. George was the younger son of Mary, who was a slave of Moses and Susan Carver. The Carvers were not like most slave owners. They did not like slavery, but discovered that help was hard to hire on the frontier. They bought Mary from neighbors and owned only her and her two children, George and his older brother, Jim. Near the end of the Civil War, Mary and George were kidnapped by a group of men known as slave raiders. These men took Mary and George to Arkansas in hopes of selling them to the highest bidder. By then the Carvers had owned Mary for about ten years. She had been part of their household since she was thirteen years old, and the Carvers considered Mary a member of their family. Moses hired someone to go find them. The slave hunter searched in Arkansas but returned only with George.

George and Jim had become orphans. By then Moses and Susan could no longer legally own Jim or George, because after the war slavery became illegal. The Thirteenth Amendment to the U.S. Constitution ended slavery for good in December 1865. The Carvers had no children and took on the role of parents to Mary's sons.

Although the war and slavery were officially finished in 1865, both continued in the hearts of many people. From 1865 to 1877, a period known as the Reconstruction, a battle raged over how the nation would be reunited and how the freed slaves would be treated. Some wanted the freed people to have the full rights of citizenship, but others wanted to create some kind of unofficial slavery. The war had been destructive to the southern economy. Many southerners believed that they did not have enough money to pay wages to workers. In Missouri and in most of the South, numerous white people were also unwilling to treat African Americans as their equals. The Carvers were unusual in their acceptance of George and Jim into their family.

Even though George and Jim were brothers, they were very different. Jim was about five years older and was much bigger and stronger than George. Jim helped the aging Moses with the heavy work on their prosperous farm. George was not only younger and smaller than Jim, he was also sickly. While Jim did heavy physical labor out of doors, George helped Susan around the house. Indoors, George learned how to cook, sew, clean house, and do laundry. George was also given a good amount of free time, and he roamed the nearby forests and creeks examining the plant and animal life. George was a curious and intelligent child, and he developed a love of nature, especially plants. He acquired a good understanding of the needs of each plant and an ability to nurse sick plants back to health. Moses Carver and other people in Diamond Grove brought their sick plants to George, and he became known as the Plant Doctor.

Diamond Grove was a tiny, rural town that had only a small general store, a blacksmith shop, a post office, and a church that doubled as a school. Fewer than twenty African Americans lived in the township. On Sundays, George and Jim were allowed to worship at the church. The church had too few members to afford a permanent pastor, so the boys listened to a wide variety of preachers from different denominations. George was greatly influenced by his religious training and developed a deep belief in what he called the Creator. He remained open to all denominations and went regularly to a variety of churches after he grew up. George believed that the Creator supplied everything that people needed, if only they would open their eyes to the bounty the Creator provided. This faith remained important to George until the day he died.

George also learned another, sadder lesson in that church building. Although the church was open to George on Sunday, he was not allowed into the building during the week when the church was used as a schoolhouse. George was clearly the smartest child in the neighborhood, but because his skin was dark he could not go to school with the white children. In the nineteenth century, few places in the South or the Midwest allowed black children and white children to go to school together. Many towns had separate schools for black children. Usually these schools received much less money from the government than the ones for white children.

Diamond Grove was too small to support two schools, so black children had no local school to attend. The Carvers could teach Jim most of what he wanted to know, but George had no outlet for his curiosity. He kept asking questions that the Carvers could not answer. Moses and Susan hired tutors to teach George at home. They could not find anyone, however, who knew enough to answer all of his questions. Carver later remembered, "I wanted to know the name of every stone and flower and insect and bird and beast. I wanted to know where it got its color, where it got its life— but there was no one to tell me."

At about the age of twelve, George left his home to go to school. The trip turned out to be longer than he expected. To gain enough education, George had to move many times to several states in the Midwest. At each new location, he hoped that he would find better educational opportunities.

George's first stop on the journey was Neosho, Missouri, about 8 miles (12.9 km) from Diamond Grove. This town was known to have a school for black children. Although George might have been scared to live so far from home, his desire to learn overcame his fear. The domestic skills he had learned from Susan proved to be valuable. A black family in Neosho took him into their home in return for his doing chores.

George used a wooden-framed slate when he attended elementary school. As paper and pencils were still expensive, students in rural areas practiced their penmanship and math sums on slates with a slate pencil. Slate is a stone that is composed of thin layers. These layers of slate were separated, trimmed, and then framed so that a child could hold them.

In Mariah and Andrew Watkins's home, George lived among other African Americans, besides his brother Jim, for the first time. He was excited to attend the tiny, one-room school for black children, where he would finally get his questions answered. Unfortunately, he was soon disappointed. Because teaching slaves to read and write had been illegal in most states, many black teachers were not highly educated themselves. These men and women worked hard to teach the freed blacks to read and write. However, few could meet the needs of gifted children such as George. His teacher was no exception. After a year in Neosho, George realized that he would have to keep looking even farther from home to find someone who was able to answer his questions.

3. Seeking an Education

No obstacle could prevent George Washington Carver from getting the education he desired, but the search was much harder than he expected. When he heard of a family moving to Fort Scott, Kansas, Carver hitched a ride with them in the late 1870s, hoping there would be a better school there. At that time many African Americans were moving to Kansas because they had few opportunities at home. Some black leaders encouraged people to come, and they described the state in glowing terms. They called Kansas the "home of John Brown." John Brown was a white abolitionist from Kansas who was hanged after leading an unsuccessful slave revolt in Harpers Ferry, Virginia, in 1859.

Many black men and women moved to Kansas expecting to be welcomed. From 1870 to 1880, the black population of the state increased from 17,000 to 43,000. The rapidly growing number of African Americans angered many whites, because black and white workers competed for scarce jobs.

John Brown's rebellion at Harpers Ferry is the subject of this 1859 wood engraving. U.S. Marines are depicted using a ladder as a battering ram to smash open the doors of the engine house. John Brown's band of raiders, inside, are shown firing at the marines through several holes in the doors.

Carver did not have too much trouble finding work. The skills Susan Carver had taught him proved useful once more. Similar to many frontier areas, Kansas had more men than women. In exchange for cooking and other chores, Carver lived with the family of a black-smith. Carver also did laundry for the guests at the Wilder House hotel, the only brick building in town.

Like Missouri, Kansas had been divided over the issue of slavery. Kansas might have been the state where John Brown lived, but Fort Scott was not his hometown.

In fact most of Fort Scott's residents were proslavery set-tlers and had detested Brown, who had sought to lure antislavery settlers to the state. Both proslavery and antislavery settlers wanted to dominate the state, and both resorted to violence to achieve their goals. In 1856, John Brown had led a raid on a proslavery town, after proslavery settlers had raided an antislavery town. Angered at the subsequent death of five settlers, proslav-ery supporters in Fort Scott had organized an unsuc-cessful attempt to capture John Brown and his followers. The town remained dominated by people who did not want slavery to end. This was not a good place for a black man looking for an education.

Carver knew about prejudice. He had not been able to attend the school in Diamond Grove because of his color. However, he was unprepared for what he wit-nessed on the night of March 26, 1879. A crowd of about one thousand people watched as thirty masked men took a black prisoner from the local jail. The prisoner had been arrested only that day and had not yet stood trial for his alleged crime. The mob did not want to wait for justice in the courts. They cheered as men tied a rope around the prisoner's neck, dragged him five blocks, hanged him from a lamppost, and set him on fire. This kind of terrible violence happened frequently after the Reconstruction, especially in the South. Although lynch-ing had originated in frontier areas without established court systems, some whites continued to use lynching as

After the Civil War, the citizens of Fort Scott, Kansas, encouraged the development of the transcontinental railroad in the West. The railroad made it possible to ship cattle and crops such as wheat from Kansas to the markets of the eastern United States. This stereograph of Fort Scott was taken by the Tresslar Brothers studio around 1870.

a way to keep African Americans powerless. The number of lynchings peaked in the 1890s, when more than one thousand black people were lynched.

"As young as I was," Carver declared more than sixty years later, "the horror haunted me and does even now." He immediately left Fort Scott for Olathe, Kansas, where Carver moved in with a black couple, Lucy and Ben Seymour, and did odd jobs while attending school. When the Seymours left about a year later for Minneapolis, Kansas, Carver went with them. His four years in Minneapolis were good ones. Carver opened a laundry and attended a two-story school with white classmates. By this time, he had acquired some additional skills. Carver impressed his teacher and the other students with not only his knowledge but also his painting and musical abilities. He often played the accordion or the harmonica at school programs.

Late in 1884, Carver moved to Kansas City, Kansas, where he learned to type and got a job as a clerk at the Union Depot. There he discovered once again that it

The Lexington Laundry of Richmond, Virginia, shown here in a photo from around 1899, was a business run by African Americans. Around the turn of the century, segregation often extended to the washing of clothes and sheets and it was not uncommon for laundries to display signs that read "We Wash For White People Only."

This family, photographed in 1897, waits for a steamboat to take them across a river on their journey to Kansas. Many black immigrants to the West paid in advance for a guide to arrange their means of travel. Unfortunately, some of these guides were con men and the families were left waiting for a boat or a wagon that never arrived.

was confusing and difficult to be black in the late nineteenth century. Although Carver was often invited into the homes of numerous white friends, he was refused service at a lunch counter in Kansas City while his white friend was permitted to stay. His friend, however, walked out with Carver. The incident was a painful reminder that, no matter how talented and courteous Carver was, some people would reject him simply because of his color. About a year later, Carver received another such reminder.

Carver heard about a small college in Highland, Kansas, and applied for admission by mail. He was thrilled to be accepted and excitedly went to the Highland College campus. When Carver arrived, however, he was turned away simply because he was black. Carver was so hurt and discouraged that for several years he gave up on the idea of going to college.

He remained in Highland and worked for a white family, once again doing chores and laundry. One of the family's sons moved to Ness County on the western plains of Kansas, and he encouraged Carver to follow him. The federal government was giving away land on the Kansas frontier, to encourage people to settle there. The Homestead Act of 1862 allowed settlers to claim 160 acres (64.8 ha) of land if they lived on it for five years and paid a fee of $24. Known as homesteaders, these people usually built sod houses made of grass and dirt, because wood was scarce on the grassy plains. In August 1886, Carver became a homesteader in Ness County, Kansas, and completed the construction of his own sod house in April 1887. His only pieces of furniture were a cookstove, a bed, a cupboard, a table, chairs, and the laundry equipment that had provided him with income for so long. Carver farmed his plot and also worked for another homesteader.

While he was in Ness County, Carver took art lessons, joined a literary society, played the accordion at local dances, and continued to collect various kinds of plants in small pots. Even as a child Carver had dug up plants and moved them to his own garden plot. By this time his collection of plants numbered more than five hundred. His many talents impressed his white neighbors. A local newspaper noted that his knowledge of plants and minerals was remarkable and called him "a man of more than ordinary ability." As did many homesteaders, however, Carver became restless.

Leaving Ness County in 1888, Carver continued his wandering. He ended up in Winterset, Iowa, sometime between 1888 and 1890. Once again he opened a laundry, attended numerous churches in his community, and became friends with local whites. His religion not only brought him comfort but also allowed him to meet

Frederick J. Bandholtz took this photograph of Simpson College around 1907. The college, which was founded in 1860 in Indianola, Iowa, welcomed students of all races. George Washington Carver would be the second African American to attend the small college.

prominent families. At one church he met Dr. and Mrs. John Milholland. Mrs. Milholland became like a mother to Carver. Both Milhollands admired Carver's paintings as well as his intelligence. They encouraged him to enroll in Simpson College, 20 miles (32.2 km) away in Indianola, Iowa. Once again he was accepted into a college, but Simpson College, unlike Highland College, actually let Carver remain once he entered its doors on September 9, 1890.

4. In College at Last

George Washington Carver had left Diamond Grove as a preteen adolescent to find an education. By the time he arrived at Simpson College, he was a young man in his mid-twenties. He was not only older than most of his fellow students but also he was the only African American. Nevertheless, he felt welcome on campus and made many friends. "They made me believe I was a real human being," he later said.

Carver's acceptance by Simpson College students and faculty was based on a number of factors. First, his devout faith in the Creator was appreciated in this Methodist school. Second, his academic, artistic, and musical abilities were far too outstanding to be ignored. Third, he had spent most of his life among whites, felt comfortable in their presence, and worked hard to make them feel comfortable around him. One female student at Simpson remembered how Carver would walk to the other side of the street when he saw any of the campus women accompanied by strangers. Carver probably didn't want the women to feel awkward when they greeted him, should the strangers at their side feel bothered by his presence. Finally, Carver had the kind of personality that drew people to him. Carver made other people feel special and important. His gift for making friends was one reason he was able to accomplish so much during his life.

Although he later became known as a scientist, Carver initially wanted to be an artist. He enrolled in the fine arts department at Simpson and impressed one of his teachers, Etta Budd. She believed that he was quite talented and said that "painting was in him."

This 1890 photograph shows Carver during an art class at Simpson College. Carver particularly enjoyed doing studies of a flowering bulb called the amaryllis. He tended an amaryllis in his room and carried the plant to his painting class.

However, she did not think that a black man could make enough money as an artist. After Carver showed her some plants he had grown, she realized that his knowledge of plants could bring him far more success. She knew of the available opportunities because her father was a professor of horticulture who taught his students how to grow plants.

Joseph Lancaster Budd taught at the nearby Iowa State College of Agriculture and Mechanic Arts, which later became Iowa State University, in Ames, Iowa. The Budds convinced Carver to transfer from Simpson to Iowa State to study botany and learn all about plants. At first Carver was afraid that he had made a mistake. He did not feel at home on this larger campus. Once again Carver was the only black student. He was also the target of unkind remarks, and some people called him names. Carver could not live in the dorm with other students and had to eat in the basement of the dining room. Before too long, however, Carver's winning personality won

Joseph Lancaster Budd, shown above, ran a nursery in Iowa before becoming a professor of horticulture at Iowa State in 1877. A nursery is a place where plants are raised and then sold to farmers or gardeners for transplanting.

him respect and affection on campus.

Carver became involved in campus activities, including the debate club and the Young Men's Christian Association (YMCA). Carver even became a captain in the campus military regiment and published a poem in the student newspaper. At the same time, he continued his hobbies of knitting, needlework, painting, and playing the accordion, as well as the guitar. George Washington Carver's talents impressed everyone. In December 1892, some students encouraged Carver to enter his paintings in an exhibit of Iowa artists at Cedar Rapids, Iowa. When Carver insisted that he could not afford the trip, his fellow students raised money to buy him a new suit and a train ticket. They

This 1894 portrait shows Carver as a quartermaster of Iowa State College's military regiment. A quartermaster is responsible for outfitting a military unit with supplies. The photograph appeared in the 1895 edition of the *Bomb*, the college's yearbook.

were thrilled when Carver's painting *Yucca and Cactus* was selected to represent Iowa at the World's Columbian Exposition in Chicago, Illinois. Visitors from all over the world came to this gigantic fair and saw Carver's painting.

His fellow students were amazed at all Carver accomplished, especially as he also worked a number of jobs to pay his way through college. These included working in the dining hall and serving as a trainer for athletic teams. Carver helped to keep the athletes in good condition through massage and exercise. To make ends meet, Carver made many of his clothes, ate wild

Frances Benjamin Johnston photographed the Palace of Mechanic Arts at the World's Columbian Exposition in Chicago, Illinois, in 1892. The 1893 fair was attended by more than 21 million visitors who marveled at innovations and attractions such as electricity and the Ferris wheel.

plants and mushrooms, and took his notes with pencil stubs that other students had thrown away.

Carver excelled in his classes, especially botany and horticulture, and was widely recognized as the best botany student on campus. Only a year and a half after starting school, Carver published the article "Grafting the Cacti" in the journal of the Iowa Horticultural Society. Many of the faculty considered Carver more their peer than their student. When he graduated, the faculty asked him to stay on as a graduate student and teach botany to first-year students. The young man who had been forced to eat in the basement became the first black faculty member of one of the nation's best agricultural colleges.

Iowa State was at the forefront of agricultural research and education in the 1890s. The college had the finest faculty of that day. In fact two of Carver's teachers later held the highest agricultural post in America, secretary of agriculture. One of them, James Wilson, noted that Carver was "by all means the ablest student we have here." He claimed that Carver's work was even better than that of the faculty "in special lines [of research] in which he has a taste." Those lines were two of the newest and most exciting areas of botanical research of that era. The first was mycology, or the study of fungus, including mushrooms and some kinds of plant diseases. The college's leading professor of mycology, L. H. Pammel, noted Carver's "instinct for

Professor James Wilson, photographed by Frances B. Johnston around 1906, later became the U.S. secretary of agriculture.

nature," which allowed Carver to spot likely locations for various kinds of fungi. Carver found several new species, and Pammel called him "the best collector I ever had in the department or have ever known."

The second of Carver's special abilities was hybridization. This scientific method attempted to make better plants by combining different kinds of plants through cross-fertilization and grafting. Carver compared hybridization to an artist mixing paints to get new colors. He noted that "man is simply nature's agent or employee to assist her in her work." Carver remained both a scientist and an artist and combined science and nature in ways few are able to do.

While he was a postgraduate student studying for his master's degree in agriculture, Carver worked in the campus greenhouse. In this large, enclosed, glass building, plants could be grown year-round. Here Carver learned even more about how to raise all kinds of plants successfully. He also taught botany to first-year students and soon became one of their favorite teachers. One of his students became a professor at the University of Wisconsin, and he later wrote Carver a

For centuries human beings grew plants to eat without understanding much about how they grew or reproduced. By the 1800s, scientists were finally learning how plants functioned. This knowledge allowed people to develop techniques to grow improved vegetables and fruit. One technique was hybridization, or the combination of two plants to create a new one.

One way to hybridize plants is through cross-fertilization. Plants create pollen, which is necessary to make new plants. In cross-fertilization people take the pollen from one plant and put it on a different plant. The new plant would then combine the qualities of both plants. An example is a tangelo, which is made from an orange, a tangerine, and a grapefruit. Another tool is grafting, or attaching a limb from one plant onto another plant. For example, through grafting, people can create trees that have white flowers on some branches and pink ones on others.

letter expressing his gratitude and noting that Carver had been his best teacher because he had guided students to discover things for themselves.

Carver's humor and love of nature were contagious. He also inspired people outside of the classroom. The six-year-old son of one professor often went with Carver on his long, daily walks in the woods, where Carver would collect plant specimens. That boy was named Henry Wallace, and he later became not only the secretary of agriculture but also the vice president of the United States. Wallace said of Carver, "He could cause a little boy to see the things which he [Carver] saw in a grass flower."

Carver continued to excel in research and published a number of articles, both in horticulture and in the field of mycology. As he finished his work for his master's degree in agriculture in 1896, two southern black colleges approached him with job offers. Carver had come to another fork in the road. He could stay among whites in Iowa and engage in cutting-edge agricultural research, or go to work among other African Americans in the poorest part of the nation, the rural South. Carver chose what he knew would be the harder path.

5. To Be of the Greatest Good

In March 1896, George Washington Carver received an important letter. This letter contained a job offer from Booker T. Washington, the president of Tuskegee Normal and Industrial Institute, which later became Tuskegee University.

Booker T. Washington had been a slave until about the age of ten, when emancipation freed him. His family was poor, and Washington worked as a miner while going to night school until he entered Hampton Normal and Agricultural Institute in Virginia. In 1881, Washington founded Tuskegee Institute in Macon County, Alabama. By 1896, both Washington and Tuskegee were famous. Washington made Tuskegee the largest and richest school to be run and staffed entirely by African Americans. Whites had established most of the other colleges for black southerners after the Civil War. Such schools as Fisk University and Howard University had white presidents and many white teachers. Most whites still believed that the former slaves were unable to take care of themselves. A

Booker T. Washington, photographed around 1900, was motivated to establish Tuskegee by the sound education he had received at the Hampton Institute. "At Hampton, I found an opportunity for class-room education and for practical training in industrial life . . . I was surrounded by . . . a spirit of self-help that seemed to awaken every faculty in me and cause me for the first time to realize what it means to be a man instead of a piece of property."

The faculty of the Tuskegee Institute was photographed in this group portrait. In the first row, Booker T. Washington is seated at center and George Washington Carver is shown fourth from the right.

successfully operated all-black school could prove such people wrong. Therefore Washington wished to hire only African Americans to work in his school.

Washington wanted to establish a department of agriculture at Tuskegee. Only one African American had the training and ability to run such a department. That person was George Washington Carver, who also had offers from Iowa State and Alcorn Agricultural and Mechanical College in Mississippi. Washington begged Carver to come and wrote, "If we cannot secure you we shall be forced perhaps to put in a white man." He also offered Carver a generous salary and agreed to let Carver finish his master's degree before coming to Tuskegee.

Although Carver was tempted to stay where he was known and respected, he felt that he must leave Iowa. Most black men and women who were able to get a college education in that difficult era believed they should share their good fortune. Carver agreed with this philosophy. He wrote to Washington that "it has always been the one ideal of my life to be of the greatest good to the greatest number of 'my people' possible." Carver declared that agricultural education was "the key to unlock the golden door of freedom to our people." Thus Carver chose to leave the security of Iowa and head south.

In 1896, the South could be a dangerous place to be black. The problems caused by Carver's color were more serious in places such as rural Alabama than they were in the Midwest. After the Civil War, the federal government had taken steps to protect the rights of the emancipated slaves and other African Americans. During the Reconstruction three constitutional amendments were passed that ended legal slavery, granted black people the right of citizenship, and forbade the states from denying the right to vote on the basis of "race, color, or previous condition of servitude." As a result, many African Americans prospered. However, their success angered many white southerners who wanted complete power over their black neighbors. Such whites sought to get the federal government to stop protecting black rights. By 1896, they had succeeded.

Without federal protection, black southerners saw their rights disappear. Southern states first found ways to take away the right to vote for most African Americans. Certain states required people to pay special taxes and to prove they could read and write in order to vote. These provisions were enforced against black voters but not against white voters. With little political power, African Americans could not stop whites from restoring a kind of slavery. Whites passed segregation laws, which required black people to be separated from whites. "White Only" signs were meant to make blacks feel inferior to whites. When black people strongly protested, they could expect violence, especially in the South. Mobs killed about two black people per week during the 1890s. No one would jail whites who killed African Americans in this manner. Even the federal government refused to act. In 1896, the U.S. Supreme Court ruled in *Plessy v. Ferguson* that segregation was legal.

In the middle of all this violence and hatred, Booker T. Washington offered a compromise to southerners. He urged southern whites to hire blacks and to allow them to get an education so that African Americans could help restore the South to prosperity. Washington told black southerners to focus on getting an education and buying land rather than on fighting for political rights. Because

During the Reconstruction, the Fourteenth
Amendment to the Constitution was passed,
which said that states had to treat everybody
the same in making new laws. However, by 1880,
many states were passing segregation laws that
said African Americans could not use the same
schools, restaurants, and other facilities that whites
used. These laws also made black people sit in the
back of streetcars and ride in separate cars on trains.

Some people believed that the Fourteenth Amendment
did not allow for such laws. One black man, Homer
Plessy, challenged one of these laws in court.
The case, called Plessy v. Ferguson, was finally
heard by the Supreme Court. In its 1896 decision,
the Court ruled that black people could be made
to use separate facilities as long as those facilities
were as good as the ones used by whites. This "separate but equal" policy made segregation legal.
However, the facilities were seldom actually equal.
The Supreme Court changed its mind in 1954 and
ruled in Brown v. Board of Education of Topeka,
Kansas that segregation in education was illegal.

of his own success, Booker T. Washington believed that anyone who worked hard would succeed. He thought that success would eventually win African Americans not only respect but also rights from whites. Carver agreed with these ideas, as he had won acceptance and rights by hard work as well.

When Carver arrived at Tuskegee in October 1896, however, he was unprepared for the size of the obstacles African Americans faced in the area known as Black Belt Alabama. Named

Supreme Court of the United States,

This official document, recorded by a clerk of the court, contains the U.S. Supreme Court's May 1896 verdict on *Plessy v. Ferguson*. The court upheld an earlier decision by the Louisiana Supreme Court which had found Homer Plessy, an African American, guilty of sitting in a "whites-only" railroad car.

the Black Belt because of the richness of its soil, the region was where the highest number of slaves had lived. When slavery ended, the area had far more black residents than white ones. Whites were terrified to think of their former slaves dominating their government and society. Thus they fought the hardest to keep blacks "in their place," which whites believed was a position of dependence and weakness. Whites wanted African Americans to think and act as if they were inferior to whites. Any black man or woman who acted otherwise could be punished. Sometimes whites took blacks' land; other times they took their lives. Despite how talented Carver was, he had to be careful in Alabama. In 1902, Carver barely escaped an angry mob, after he had accompanied a white woman photographer to Ramer, Alabama. The northern photographer Frances B. Johnston had come to the south to do research on African American schools. Carver wrote Washington, "I had the most frightful experience of my life there and for one day and night it was a very serious question indeed as to whether I would return to Tuskegee alive or not."

Carver was also surprised by the poverty of the South. White southerners had embraced slavery because it was cheaper than paying wages to workers. Whites spent much of their money buying additional slaves and land so they could plant more cotton. Before the Civil War, high cotton prices made the South wealthy. Instead of building factories as northerners had done, southerners bought slaves. When slavery was abolished, southerners had nothing to show for all the money they had spent for slaves. Still dependent on cotton for its income, the South went from being the wealthiest region in America to being the poorest. Cotton prices were not high enough for landowners to pay workers decent wages and still make much profit. Sharecropping had become the answer.

This photograph, taken around 1899, depicts the homes of a poor African American community in Chattanooga, Tennessee. The image might have been part of the American Negro exhibit at the Paris Exposition of 1900.

Under the system of sharecropping, however, many former slaves found themselves working for little more than they had received as slaves.

Carver believed that the Creator had given him special talents to make life better for other people, especially for African Americans. When Carver came to Alabama, he thought of himself as a missionary. However, his chosen mission would be far more difficult than he had imagined.

6. A Challenging Task

George Washington Carver's move to Alabama was a challenge for many reasons. Most of the whites he had known in the Midwest had encouraged him to succeed. In the South, he had to adjust to white people who were hostile to black success. At Iowa State, Carver had learned the best methods of farming. Most of these methods were aimed at independent, landowning farmers. In Alabama, he had to work with poor sharecroppers who could not afford to use many of the methods he had learned. Finally, Carver had lived among whites most of his life. In Alabama, he had to live in a black community and had little experience in doing so.

At first Carver did not do a good job of fitting in with the faculty at Tuskegee. Carver's belief in his talents led him to feel somewhat superior to others. Because Booker T. Washington had begged him to come to Tuskegee, Carver felt himself to be an important member of the faculty. Other teachers resented this attitude as well as Carver's high salary. It took Carver longer to win acceptance and affection at Tuskegee than it had at

Simpson College and Iowa State. Indeed he found it easier to make friends among some of the area's white neighbors, who appreciated his advice on their gardens. Eventually Carver made some close friends among the faculty, but he continued to feel that he was not sufficiently appreciated by his fellow teachers.

Carver had always worked hard, but he soon learned that Booker T. Washington demanded even more from him. Washington had succeeded in large part because he was able to accomplish a lot with little money. For example, Tuskegee students not only built their own buildings but also they made the bricks to construct them. Washington expected even more from the faculty than he did the students. This impressed wealthy people, such as the industrialist and philanthropist Andrew Carnegie, who gave Washington money to operate Tuskegee. Donations such as these funded the agricultural department, which Carver was to run. In richer schools, at least five different people did the work that Carver had to do single handedly.

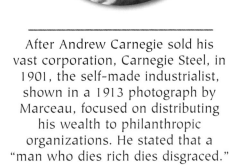

After Andrew Carnegie sold his vast corporation, Carnegie Steel, in 1901, the self-made industrialist, shown in a 1913 photograph by Marceau, focused on distributing his wealth to philanthropic organizations. He stated that a "man who dies rich dies disgraced."

Perhaps Carver's biggest job was to serve as a kind of principal to the school of agriculture. He was responsible for seeing that everything got done. Unlike most principals, however, Carver had to teach classes as well. He not only taught students in the classroom but also taught farmers in the field. The agriculture department also operated a full-scale farm, which provided much of the food that was served to the students and faculty. Carver oversaw its operations, including the planting of crops and the care of animals, as Tuskegee could not afford a veterinarian to care for sick livestock.

During the first year that Carver was on campus, Tuskegee received money to open an agricultural experiment station. On other campuses, these stations had a separate director and staff who experimented on the best methods to grow crops. They published bulletins to educate farmers about the station's findings. In the beginning, Carver was the director of Tuskegee's station and its only staff member. On top of this impossible workload, Booker T. Washington asked Carver to be responsible for keeping the school's grounds in good shape and for taking care of the school's sanitation system.

Carver not only had too much to do but also had little money to accomplish these tasks. He found no laboratory at Tuskegee for his work. Instead he created his own laboratory using equipment made from old kitchen pots and discarded wire. When he finished

Scientists, like artists, must use their creativity. Early in his career, Carver lacked the funds to purchase lab equipment. He used household objects such as a rolling pin and grater to crush plant specimens. "I went to the trash pile . . . and started my laboratory with bottles, old pint jars, and any other thing I found I could use."

writing bulletins, Carver often found that there was no money to print them. His experiment station received only a fraction of the money other stations did. Yet Washington expected Tuskegee's agricultural department and experiment station to perform as well as those with larger staffs and more money.

Washington's demands and Carver's frustrations were bound to create problems between them. Both were proud men who shared many of the same goals and beliefs. Each had great respect for the other, but the

two men were often angry with each other. Carver was an outstanding teacher and scholar. Washington, however, needed someone who could manage a farm and run a school. Carver was not good at these practical skills. He preferred research and teaching to handling the day-to-day details of farming or being a principal. When Washington gave some of these responsibilities to others, Carver felt insulted and protested. Carver did not like the idea of other people being in charge of his work, and this created a great deal of conflict.

These problems were most evident in the poultry yard. Carver had little experience in raising chickens. Although he could grow huge, healthy plants, the chickens under his care began to die. Washington wanted to give this task to George R. Bridgeforth, a newcomer who joined the agricultural department in 1902. Carver threatened to quit when Bridgeforth was promoted to head of the agricultural department in 1910, but Washington did not back down. Carver became the director of agricultural research and the experiment station. This managerial change actually freed Carver to do only those things he enjoyed. However, Carver was too proud to be happy about getting relief from an impossible workload if it meant reporting to Bridgeforth.

Previous spread: This photograph shows the chemistry lab at Tuskegee Institute. Professor Carver (_second from right_) believed that "the most effective and lasting education is the one that makes the pupil handle, discuss and familiarize himself with the real things about him. . . ."

Washington sometimes got so angry with Carver that he threatened to fire him. No matter how frustrated he got at Carver's failures, however, Washington also realized Carver's great talents. One of these was certainly Carver's classroom teaching. His humor as well as his warm personality made him a favorite of the students. They not only took his academic courses but also some gave up an hour of their free time to attend a Bible class that he taught on Sundays. One Bible student noted that in Carver's class "[for the] first time in my life I was witnessing no gloom surrounding the Bible." In the Bible class, Carver explained that "our Creator is the same and

This photograph of the Tuskegee chapel was taken around 1900. In 1907 Carver began holding a weekly Bible class for about six students. Several months later voluntary attendance to this class rose to as many as 114 students. Carver taught the class until he died.

never changes despite the names given Him by people here and in all parts of the world." Carver continued, "Even if we gave Him no name at all, He would still be there, within us, waiting to give us good on this earth."

The central lesson Carver taught in all his courses was how all living things were interconnected. What happened to any plant or animal had an impact on all the others. Carver preached that the Creator provided everything that was needed. People could destroy the Creator's work, however, if they failed to understand and use these resources wisely. To illustrate this idea, Carver sometimes showed his students tangled, dirty strings in one of his hands while in the other hand he held string that had been cleaned, tied, and neatly wound together into a ball. Then Carver would tell them that the tangled mess was ignorance and that the ball represented the order that a wise use of resources could bring.

Carver described learning as the process of "understanding relationships." He believed a teacher should lead students from what they already knew to the "nearest related unknown." Because he believed in the unity of all life, Carver would often use a single object to explain all the natural forces. For example, he brought a pea plant to class and described everything that played a role in making that specific plant live and grow. Rather than teaching chemistry in one class and botany in another, he explained how chemical and biological forces worked together to shape the life of a single pea plant. This method of learning made it easier for his students to grasp how the same processes worked in other plants and animals. They learned to love nature from their teacher.

Many students also learned to love Carver as a second father. Carver knew many of his students well because he lived in an apartment in Rockefeller Hall, the boys' dorm. Some students wrote to him for advice and help many years after they had graduated from Tuskegee. The students felt comfortable sharing their fears and dreams with Carver. One former student complained that, although he was trying to be like

This photograph of the grounds of the Tuskegee Normal and Industrial Institute was taken around 1916.

Carver, Carver kept achieving more than the student could match. The student wrote Carver, "Now young man I'm getting good and tired of it and if you want me to follow you any further you'll just have to slow down to some reasonable pace that's all!!"

Washington was wise to hold on to a man who could inspire students as Carver did. As director of agricultural research and the experiment station, Carver would use his ability to motivate others by educating farmers outside of the classroom as well.

7. The Experiment Station and Teaching Farmers

Iowa State had trained George Washington Carver to be an agricultural researcher, not a farmer. He soon learned, however, that research was not a priority to Washington. The principal knew that the whole world was looking at Tuskegee. Many would judge the ability of African Americans by the college's success. Washington was more concerned with how the chicken yard looked than whether Carver discovered a new species of fungus. Nevertheless, Washington wanted Tuskegee's agricultural experiment station to compare well to all the other stations. This proved to be quite a challenge.

During the mid-nineteenth century, farming had become more scientific. Congress wanted to help farmers learn the newest methods. In 1862, Congress gave the states land to sell, the profits from which were to be used to fund the building of agricultural colleges. These state schools, such as Iowa State, were called land-grant colleges. Next Congress passed the Hatch Act in 1887, to provide these colleges with money for agricultural research. The land-grant colleges opened agricultural

After the first land-grant act, the Morrill Act, was passed in 1862, most of the land-grant colleges in the South refused to allow black students to attend. To get a good agricultural education, an African American had to go to a northern school, such as Iowa State. In 1890, some people in Congress felt that this was unfair and that something should be done. Congress passed another Morrill Act to provide funding for states to open agricultural colleges for black southerners. The seventeen schools that opened were called the 1890 schools. Like most segregated institutions, these colleges got significantly less money than did the original, whites-only land-grant schools.

experiment stations. At first no black schools received these federal funds. In 1896, Tuskegee became the first black school to open an agricultural experiment station.

At that time, black schools usually received far less money from the government than did white schools. In 1896, the white school in nearby Auburn, Alabama, received $15,000 of Hatch funds. Tuskegee received only $1,500 from state funds. In addition, the Auburn station got money from other sources. In 1912, it received almost $70,000, while the Tuskegee station still got only $1,500 from the state. Sometimes Booker T. Washington diverted part of that amount for other things that he considered more important.

Tuskegee students are shown working in the fields of the school's experiment station. To increase the number of agricultural students, Carver had several suggestions for Washington in 1906: Wooden boards should be put up to protect students from storms, successful professionals should lecture students about their trade, and students should be rewarded for the long days they spent tending their plots.

Because Carver received no money from the federal government, the U.S. Department of Agriculture might have ignored his station. Fortunately, one of Carver's former professors, James Wilson, had become the U.S. secretary of agriculture in 1897. Wilson made sure that Carver's station was included in his department's reports and mailings. At first Alfred C. True, the director of the Office of Experiment Stations, thought Carver had made a mistake when he reported receiving only $1,500. True found it hard to believe that any station could operate with so little money. As the only black-run experiment station included in the reports, the Tuskegee station and its director became well known to other researchers. Carver also received reports of their activities.

With so little money, Carver's station could not undertake many of the projects other stations did, which turned out to be a good thing. Too much of what the other stations produced was aimed at educated and rich farmers who owned their own land. Sharecroppers could not afford to try expensive fertilizers or to buy costly equipment. They needed methods that were inexpensive. Carver's station supplied that need.

For example, the Tuskegee station taught farmers how to enrich their soil without using store-bought fertilizer. Carver encouraged sharecroppers to use a variety of methods. One was to compost by saving food scraps and animal waste to add to the soil. Another was called green manuring, which used the nutrients in plants themselves to improve the land. Carver encouraged farmers to alternate between cotton and other crops, such as peas and beans, which enriched the soil. Pea and bean plants could be plowed into the soil after harvest. After the plants decayed over the winter, the remains acted very much like a fertilizer. Neither method would cost the sharecropper a penny.

The aim of agricultural research was to try out new methods to help farmers succeed in producing better crops. These methods could not help the farmers unless

> *Carver thought certain materials were ideal for composting: "Weeds, grass, leaves, pine tag, wood ashes, old plaster, lime, old clothing, shoes, broken up bones, feathers, hair, horns and hoofs of animals, swamp muck, etc., should go into the compost heap." After these items had decayed, their rotten remains could then be used as fertilizer.*

they knew about them. This meant that experiment stations had to find ways to let farmers know what had been learned. Efforts to teach farmers became known as outreach programs. The major tool of most experiment stations was the publication of bulletins. The stations, Carver's included, printed their findings in pamphlets to be distributed to farmers.

Because bulletins were the most visible evidence of a station's success, Booker T. Washington wanted Carver to publish as many as other stations did. This was an unfair expectation. By 1905, the Auburn station employed thirteen well-educated men, who all wrote its bulletins.

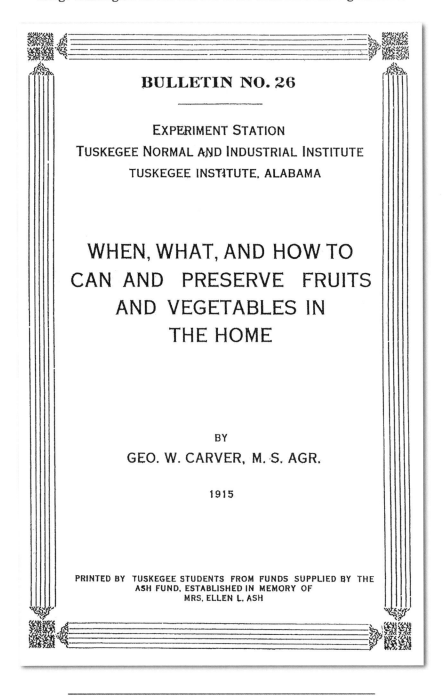

BULLETIN NO. 26

EXPERIMENT STATION
TUSKEGEE NORMAL AND INDUSTRIAL INSTITUTE
TUSKEGEE INSTITUTE, ALABAMA

WHEN, WHAT, AND HOW TO CAN AND PRESERVE FRUITS AND VEGETABLES IN THE HOME

BY

GEO. W. CARVER, M. S. AGR.

1915

PRINTED BY TUSKEGEE STUDENTS FROM FUNDS SUPPLIED BY THE
ASH FUND, ESTABLISHED IN MEMORY OF
MRS. ELLEN L. ASH

This 1915 bulletin instructed farmers on how to preserve their harvested fruits and vegetables. Produce such as tomatoes and peaches spoil in a short time. By learning how to can and preserve safely, farmers could keep their cupboards stocked until the next harvest.

Carver wrote twenty-nine of the thirty-one bulletins that the Tuskegee station published between 1896 and 1916. None of the Auburn researchers had nearly as many other duties as Carver had.

Bulletins could benefit those farmers who had the ability and the time to read them. Many of the share-croppers in the South had neither. Some of the bulletins of other stations also seemed to have been written for other researchers, not for actual farmers. Even educated white farmers often came to Tuskegee to ask Carver to explain the content of other stations' bulletins. Carver tried to keep most of his bulletins simple enough to be understood by people with a limited education. Carver also knew that bulletins could not reach everyone, and he tried other methods of outreach as well.

Tuskegee sponsored a farmers' fair and an annual meeting, which allowed farmers to gather to share their successes and failures. A main purpose of the meeting was to inspire sharecroppers to buy their own land. The sharecroppers received more than inspiration, however. They were also given the means to accomplish that goal. At these gatherings, Carver and other instructors gave the farmers suggestions and even new seeds to try. Farmers learned how to save money in order to buy land.

Yearly gatherings were not enough. There was too much to be taught in one day. Tuskegee began to host Farmers' Institutes, which were free minischools held

Frances B. Johnston took this 1906 photo of Carver holding a piece of soil. When Carver began experimenting with clay paints, he wrote to Washington that he was eager to dig on Tuskegee's land to find suitable clay.

at night so that share-croppers could come after they finished all their chores. Farmers who did not have the time or the money to enroll in Tuskegee could attend these classes at night. George Washington Carver and other instructors taught them ways to improve both their crops and their lives. For example, share-croppers learned how to make paint from native clays so that they could paint their homes.

However, many farmers were too tired or lived too far away to get to Tuskegee. From the time he arrived on campus, Carver had used his weekends to travel to farms and rural churches to reach such people. Eventually other instructors were hired to do the same thing. They were called demonstration agents, because they showed farmers how to do things instead of just telling them how.

In 1906, Tuskegee became one of the first colleges to create a movable school. With money given by a

New York banker named Morris K. Jesup, Tuskegee turned a wagon into a classroom on wheels. The wagon carried all kinds of farming equipment as well as pictures and charts to teach better farming methods. Farmers working in cotton fields would look up and find what was called the Jesup Wagon parked at the end of the row, ready to bring them the benefits of scientific agriculture.

Another important outreach tool was the work of Carver's students after they returned to their homes. Tuskegee urged its graduates to use their education not merely to enrich themselves but also to better the lives

Demonstration agents and a nurse stand alongside the movable school in this 1923 photo by G. W. Ackerman. The first Jesup Agricultural Wagon, built by Tuskegee students in 1906, was pulled by a horse. By 1930, the contents of the Jesup Wagon were housed within a truck.

of less fortunate African Americans. Carver's former students often became teachers themselves, and some even opened their own schools. Through their efforts and Tuskegee's other outreach programs, hundreds of black sharecroppers discovered ways to improve the lives of their families.

8. Carver's Message for the South

Although George Washington Carver had resented George Bridgeforth's becoming head of Tuskegee's agricultural department in 1910, the change gave Carver more time to confront the problems of the South. At the beginning of the twentieth century, many people realized that the South had to change its ways or remain poor. Cotton crops did not bring in enough money to provide good homes and food for everyone. Many landowners, bankers, merchants, and sharecroppers depended on a high price for cotton to prosper. When prices were low, landowners planted more cotton in order to make enough money. This created so much cotton that the landowners got paid even less for their crop as the supply outweighed the demand. Because cotton had made the South wealthy before the Civil War, many southerners stubbornly refused to try other crops or to invest their money in building factories.

At the same time, cotton plants removed a lot of good things from the soil in order to grow. If a farmer planted

The cotton plant produces flowers that fall off and are replaced by bolls. These bolls are small capsules that contain seeds with long hairs. The hairs are later spun into cotton threads. Charles Napier Lochman photographed this cotton plant around 1896.

cotton on his land for too many years, his soil would no longer grow anything. That is one of the reasons farmers paid so much for fertilizers, as fertilizers allowed them to keep growing cotton year after year. However, store-bought fertilizers usually lasted for only a short period of time. Therefore, southern farmers spent a lot of money to keep their soil fertile, which is one reason they did not make enough money from growing cotton.

At harvest time, sharecroppers had to give all the cotton they had grown to the landowner. He sold the crop and paid himself first. Then he paid any banker or store owner from whom the sharecroppers had borrowed. When cotton prices were low, there often was no money left for the sharecroppers. After a year of hard work, the sharecroppers had to borrow still more money to feed their families. Debt became a trap. Because sharecropping families were unable to make a decent living, many people in the South were sick and hungry.

The plight of the sharecroppers saddened George Washington Carver. He believed several things had to change. First, the South had to quit depending on cotton and find new crops. Second, farmers had to stop relying on commercial fertilizers. Third, sharecroppers needed help to get out of debt and buy their own land. Finally, everyone needed to learn how to use and take care of the gifts that nature provided.

One of the things that plants need for growth is an element called nitrogen. Cotton plants took nitrogen from the soil and used it all up. Carver learned that a number of crops got their nitrogen from the air and actually put nitrogen back into the soil. Among these beneficial plants were peanuts and black-eyed peas. Carver encouraged farmers to rotate their crops by planting cotton one year and other plants such as peanuts the next. By doing this farmers could break their dependence on both cotton and expensive commercial fertilizers.

Carver liked these plants for another reason. People were just beginning to learn how important it was to eat healthy foods. Many southerners were sick from not getting the right foods. Pellagra, one of the diseases related to poor nutrition, resulted from a diet that lacked key vitamins. The disease gave people sores on their skin, upset their stomachs, and made them feel tired. Carver encouraged farmers to plant gardens with different kinds of

The peanut plant belongs to a large family of related plants called legumes. Other legumes are peas and kidney beans. The scientific name for the peanut plant is *Arachis hypogaea*.

vegetables in order to get the necessary vitamins.

George Washington Carver found that sweet potatoes were especially good for people. In addition, potatoes could be stored to last through the winter. Sharecroppers could eat the potatoes instead of buying food on credit.

People also need protein in order to build muscles. Meat is the richest source of protein, but most sharecroppers could not afford to buy it. Peanuts provided protein. By planting peanuts to eat as well as to sell, poor farmers could become healthier without having to borrow money to buy meat, eggs, and milk. Being sick made it difficult for farmers to succeed, get out of debt, and buy land. Poor southerners, both black and white, were often called lazy. Most of these individuals were sick, not lazy.

To get more people to plant peanuts, sweet potatoes, and other crops, Carver published bulletins that focused on a specific plant. Carver described the nature of the plant, how to plant it, and also how to use it. He included recipes showing how to cook the crop in a variety of ways. *Cow Peas*, a bulletin that Carver published in 1903, had recipes for what would later be called black-eyed peas. Carver published a similar bulletin about sweet potatoes in 1910. One of his most famous bulletins, *How to Grow the Peanut and 105 Ways of Preparing It for Human Consumption*, was published in 1916.

Farmers responded and began to grow less cotton and more peanuts and other crops. At first, however, farmers had a hard time selling what they did not eat. Some farmers came and complained to Carver about the low prices they got for peanuts and sweet potatoes. Carver began researching alternative uses of the crops other than their use as food. He started making such things as ink from peanut shells. Eventually, Carver claimed to have created more than three hundred peanut products.

Carver had two reasons for creating so many peanut products. First, he wanted to get more people to buy the farmers' crops. Second, he wanted poor sharecroppers to make more things for themselves. If sharecroppers were more self-reliant, they wouldn't have to borrow as much money. To show people the uses of peanuts and other crops, Carver created large displays of the hundreds of

BULLETIN NO. 31   JUNE 1925

How to Grow the Peanut and 105 Ways of Preparing it for Human Consumption

Seventh Edition
January 1940

By
GEORGE W. CARVER, M. S. in AGR.
Director

EXPERIMENTAL STATION
TUSKEGEE INSTITUTE
Tuskegee Institute, Alabama

This is the cover from the 1940 seventh edition of Carver's popular bulletin on peanuts. The bulletin had many peanut recipes, which included soup, cookies, butter, macaroni and cheese, pudding, and tutti-frutti caramels.

products he had made. His artistic abilities allowed him to make these exhibits impressive.

Because Carver was an artist, he wanted poor people to have more than just food and shelter. He sought to find ways to bring beauty in their lives, too. Struggling just to survive, sharecroppers could not afford to buy art or flowers. They did not have the money even to paint their houses, which were often only one-room shacks. Carver promised to help the farmer make "his surroundings more healthful, more cheerful, and more beautiful, thus bringing a joy and comfort into his home that he has not known heretofore."

As always, Carver looked for answers in the things nature provided for free. He discovered that southern soil often contained natural clays. In a bulletin published in 1911, Carver taught people how to make paints out of the clay they found all around them. He also experimented with wild plants to observe which ones could be dug up and transplanted into yards. Farmers could make their homes much prettier without paying a cent.

Carver added the clay products to his exhibit. He began to become famous for his many inventions. People from all over the South and the Midwest asked Carver to bring his exhibit to their state fairs and other events. Farmers' groups asked him to speak at their gatherings. Carver was very good at getting people's attention and entertaining them. One listener wrote to Carver, "You are the most seductive being I know, capable of making yourself loved by all the world when you choose." When people heard that Carver was coming, men and women crowded in to see him. Many whites also began to attend his talks. In 1903, the president of the University of Georgia heard Carver speak and declared, "That was the best lecture on agriculture to which it has ever been my privilege to listen." Such responses made Booker T. Washington especially glad that he had not fired Carver, who used his great ability and popularity to enrich both sharecroppers and the South as a whole.

9. The Wizard of Tuskegee

Until he died on November 14, 1915, Booker T. Washington was the most famous black man alive. He accomplished so much that he became known as the Wizard of Tuskegee. Many whites considered Washington to be the leader of his fellow African Americans. People all over the world knew of him and Tuskegee Institute. Some people gave money to the school because they liked him. Washington was a hard man to replace. His death had a great impact on both the school and George Washington Carver.

Robert Russa Moton became the new president of Tuskegee. Moton had been an administrator at the Hampton Normal and Agricultural Institute in Virginia since his graduation from there in 1890. Although Moton was good at running the college, he never became as well known as Washington. Carver began receiving the attention the world had once given to Washington and became the best-known African American. Many magazines and newspapers printed articles about Carver. Tuskegee Institute came to depend on Carver's celebrity status to bring fame and donations to the school. Moton encouraged Carver to travel so that more people would learn about Tuskegee. People started referring to Carver as the Wizard of Tuskegee, a nickname they had formally used for Washington.

Making more than three hundred things from the lowly peanut did seem like the work of a wizard. Moton knew that Carver was acclaimed because of this wizardry, and he freed Carver from most of his other duties at Tuskegee to allow him more time to experiment and travel. At the experiment station, Carver did two kinds of research: plot work and laboratory work. Plot work was planting a piece of land with a particular crop to find the best way to grow that crop. In the laboratory, Carver used chemicals and microscopes to investigate what the soil contained, to identify plant diseases, and to create his many products.

After 1915, Carver spent increasingly more time in the laboratory even though the lab remained poorly equipped. A number of white scientists who visited Tuskegee were astonished with Carver's lack of basic laboratory equipment, and several of the visitors donated used equipment to the school. Although Carver's college training was in agriculture, many people began to consider him a chemist and an inventor.

Carver had long felt that he was not sufficiently appreciated by Washington and others at Tuskegee.

This is the official seal of the British Royal Society to which Carver was elected a member in 1916. William Shipley had founded the society in the eighteenth century with the goal of promoting developments in the arts, the sciences, and manufacturing.

Therefore it became exceedingly important to Carver to be praised for his work. At first much of that praise came from fellow scientists, most of whom were white. In 1916, two organizations asked Carver to join them. First Carver agreed to serve on the advisory board of the National Agricultural Society. Then the British Royal Society of Arts invited him to join. Becoming a member of the Royal Society, which sought to encourage creativity and innovation, brought Carver much publicity. His rise out of slavery into membership in the Royal Society seemed truly remarkable. This society had been in existence since 1754 and was always headed by a member of the British royal family. Benjamin Franklin had also been a distinguished member of the Royal Society.

In 1917, the United States entered World War I. This conflict was the biggest war the world had ever seen. As so many people in Europe were fighting, Americans could not find enough of the products they usually bought from Europeans. Carver found substitutes for some of these products. He made dyes from vegetables to replace German dyes, and he created a kind of rubber from sweet potatoes. There were also shortages of wheat, so Carver developed flour from sweet potatoes. This caught the attention of the federal government. Scientists from the government asked Carver to come to Washington, D.C., in 1918 to share his discovery. He worked with them to perfect the flour, but the war soon ended, and wheat became plentiful again.

Carver announced in 1919 that he had created a new product from peanuts, a milk that could be used in cooking or as a beverage. This announcement caught the attention of the owners of companies that bought peanuts and packaged them for sale. Previously, Carver had worked mainly with people who grew peanuts. The peanut processors were excited to learn about his many peanut products. In 1920, Carver spoke at a national meeting of the United Peanut Association of America, which included both peanut growers and processors. Carver's speech so captivated his listeners that the following year the association paid Carver's way to go to Washington, D.C., to convince Congress to put a tariff on foreign peanuts. For such important occasions, Carver often wore the suit students at Iowa State had given him many years before. Carver did not look impressive in his old clothing, but he dazzled the congressmen with his peanut wizardry and the tariff was passed.

Numerous magazines and newspapers wrote about Carver and usually focused on his rise from slavery. Reporters would also describe his long daily morning walks in the woods and how he always wore a flower in the lapel of his coat. Readers learned about a humble man, who relied upon God for the inspiration for his many inventions. His story appealed to a variety of people.

After he became famous, Carver won a number of awards and honors. In 1923, two very different groups honored him: the United Daughters of the Confederacy (UDC), and the National Association for the Advancement of Colored People (NAACP). The UDC was dedicated to preserving the memory of the slave-owning states that had fought against the

Union. The group's president claimed, "As a southern organization, we naturally feel an interest for the negro that people of other portions of the country do not either feel or understand."

The NAACP sought to bring freedom and rights to emancipated slaves and other African Americans. The NAACP listed their reasons for honoring Carver as his "services in agricultural chemistry, his recent recognition by a British Royal Society, and for lectures on agriculture during the last year before white and colored audiences, particularly in the South, where his clear

George Washington Carver was awarded the NAACP's Spingarn Medal in 1923. The medal, which is awarded annually, honors the outstanding achievements of an African American.

The N.A.A.C.P., founded in 1909, was committed to promoting racial equality and ending lynchings against African Americans. The N.A.A.C.P. held their 1920 conference in Atlanta, Georgia. This was brave, as the Ku Klux Klan, a hate group that targeted African Americans, was especially active in that city.

thought and straightforward attitude have greatly increased inter-racial knowledge and respect."

Carver got along with so many different kinds of people for several reasons. He was a kind man who did not like to hurt people's feelings. Although he was proud, Carver acted in a humble manner. Carver's abilities and accomplishments inspired awe. His winning personality made almost everyone he met feel that he was a friend. He also avoided talking about politics. Other famous black men made public statements about issues that made people argue. Carver talked only about his work and using nature to meet the world's needs.

Some southern whites wanted to teach other southern whites to respect their black neighbors. They joined to form a group known as the Commission on Interracial Cooperation (CIC). The group's members decided that Carver would be a good person to show whites the abilities of African Americans. They paid Carver's expenses to travel to white colleges all over the South. Carver not only gave lectures but also met with individual students. Because Carver had never married or had children of his own, he had called various Tuskegee students his children. By the 1920s, Carver had added a number of white students to his family. All Carver's children wrote to him regularly for advice and help. Some of the white students became fighters for the rights of black people.

During his many lectures Carver impressed adults as well as students. Some white people offered him jobs with high salaries. The famous inventor Thomas Edison wanted Carver to work for him, but Carver turned down the offer. Carver believed he could do more to help African Americans by staying at Tuskegee. He also refused to

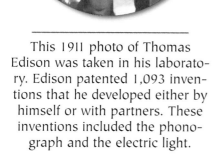

This 1911 photo of Thomas Edison was taken in his laboratory. Edison patented 1,093 inventions that he developed either by himself or with partners. These inventions included the phonograph and the electric light.

take money for the help he gave such companies as the Tom Huston Company in nearby Columbus, Georgia. Tom Huston had asked for Carver's help in finding better ways to process peanuts for sale. To express his gratitude to Carver, Huston had a bronze plaque of the professor made and donated it to Tuskegee. Huston also wanted Carver to work for him and was willing to pay Carver a high salary. Carver could certainly have earned a great deal of money, but money didn't mean much to him. Occasionally, he even stuck his paycheck in a drawer and forgot to deposit it.

A Pullman porter stands behind passengers on an Atchison, Topeka & Santa Fe Railroad Company coach car in 1905. Although black passengers sat apart from white passengers, the Pullman company employed black porters to serve guests on luxurious trains such as this one.

Not all whites were as nice to Carver as Huston was. After Carver became famous, some whites still refused to let him near them. In 1930, Carver had reserved a space in a special sleeping car for his trip to Oklahoma City, Oklahoma. However, when Carver tried to board the train he was forced to move to a segregated railroad car, even though Carver had reserved a nicer sleeping car. During a visit to New York in 1939 a New York hotel told Carver that there was no vacancy, even though Carver had reserved a room. No matter how much Carver accomplished or how nice he was, these people saw only his color and refused to accept him. The Wizard of Tuskegee did not have enough magic to cure their hatred.

10. Carver's Final Years and Legacy

As George Washington Carver began to grow older, he worried that he might be remembered for the wrong things. In the 1920s, most Americans idolized business-people and inventors. New inventions such as cars, telephones, radios, and movies greatly changed people's lives. Americans wanted all these things and admired those people who could afford to buy them. They admired even more the people who invented and produced those products, which is why they were more impressed by Carver's many inventions than by all the people he had helped. Carver recognized that he had allowed himself to be diverted from his original vision for about a decade.

Some businessmen approached Carver in the 1920s about selling his inventions. Although he had turned down earlier offers to make money from his ideas, he agreed to let these men form the Carver Products Company in 1923. Carver did not want to get rich, he just wanted everyone to value his work. Carver wanted people to think that what he had done was important. Having a company named for him would certainly impress more people than his agricultural work had. To keep others from stealing Carver's ideas, the business-men encouraged him to get three patents from the government. These government certificates forbade anyone from using the methods described in them without the consent of the inventor. The Carver Products Company did not actually make the products; it tried to get other companies to buy the ideas.

The company failed for several reasons. One was that Carver's work had been aimed at finding things to replace goods bought by poor sharecroppers. The company had a hard time selling things that people could make for themselves. Another reason was that the entire American economy collapsed in the 1930s, and the nation entered its most severe economic depression ever. Companies and banks went out of business, and many people lost their jobs.

The Great Depression of the 1930s caused Carver to return to his original vision and goals. He wanted to show all Americans how to make the most of what nature provided. Carver saw people going hungry and published the pamphlet *Some Choice Wild Vegetables that Make Fine Foods*. Carver began to realize that his lavish exhibits of products confused many viewers about his message. He turned down invitations to display them. He wrote, "This technical exhibit has no value except to interest the curious, and maybe a very few factory people."

Patented Jan. 6, 1925.   1,522,176

UNITED STATES PATENT OFFICE.

GEORGE WASHINGTON CARVER, OF TUSKEGEE, ALABAMA.

COSMETIC AND PROCESS OF PRODUCING THE SAME.

No Drawing.   Application filed September 17. 1923. Serial No. 663,302.

To all whom it may concern:

Be it known that I, GEORGE WASHINGTON CARVER, a citizen of the United States, residing at Tuskegee, in the county of Macon and State of Alabama, have invented certain new and useful Improvements in Cosmetics and Processes of Producing the Same, of which the following is a specification.

The invention relates to cosmetics and has as an object the provision of a pomade or cream made from peanuts. A further object of the invention is the provision of a process for making a pomade from peanuts which will provide a "vanishing cream" of any desired or usual tint, the pomade or cream having powder combined therewith. To carry out the process, the peanuts may be utilized in their raw, boiled or blanched condition and are first ground or macerated in any desired manner to the fineness of peanut butter. If for any reason a granular pomade is desired the grinding of the peanuts is carried out only to the extent necessary to give the character desired to the finished product. When ground to the fineness of peanut butter as suggested the resulting product will be a perfectly smooth substance.

To the ground or macerated nuts taking as a basis one ounce of peanuts there is next added 100 c. c. of pure water either hot or cold which is well stirred in with the ground nuts.

The resulting mixture is then strained through a piece of cheese cloth with gentle pressure and is put on the stove or water bath and evaporated until the oil becomes plainly visible on the surface.

The resulting product may be used unmodified in the subsequent steps or 2 c. c. of peanut oil may be added and the entire mass stirred until it becomes of the consistency of thick cream.

The material is then removed from the fire and approximately six grams of toilet powder such as kaolin, kaolinite, or china clay (preferably having slight fuller's earth properties) is added and the combined mass is thoroughly mixed until it becomes a thick heavy cream.

A quantity of salicylic acid substantially the size of a small pea, 10 drops of benzoin, and three or four drops of any desired perfume are then added. The mass thus obtained is finally ground or macerated until absolutely smooth, if the smooth product is desired, and the product is packed in porcelain, or glass containers.

If desired the above process may be modified by omitting either the added peanut oil, or the toilet powders, or both. By proper choice of the toilet powder any desired color may be given the product, from the dark brunette shades through the pinks, lavenders, to pure white.

I claim:—

1. The process of producing a cosmetic which comprises reducing peanuts to a finely divided condition, diluting the product with water reducing the mass to a consistency of thick cream and adding a preservative thereto.

2. The process of producing a cosmetic which comprises reducing peanuts to a finely divided condition, adding peanut oil and a preservative thereto and reducing the mass to a consistency of thick cream.

3. The process of producing a cosmetic which comprises reducing peanuts to a finely divided condition, diluting the product, adding toilet powder and a preservative thereto and reducing the mass to a consistency of thick cream.

4. The process of producing a cosmetic which comprises reducing peanuts to a finely divided condition, diluting with water, heating the mixture, adding peanut oil and a preservative and reducing the mass to a consistency of thick cream.

5. The process of producing cosmetics which comprises reducing peanuts to a finely divided condition, diluting the product, evaporating until oil appears upon the surface, adding peanut oil, toilet powder and a preservative.

6. The process of producing cosmetics which comprises reducing peanuts to a finely divided condition, diluting the product, straining the diluted mass, evaporating until oil appears upon the surface, adding peanut oil, stirring toilet powder into the mass, adding a preservative and a perfume and macerating until smooth.

7. The process of producing a cosmetic which comprises reducing peanuts to a finely divided condition, diluting with water, straining, evaporating until oil appears upon the surface, adding peanut oil, stirring

On January 6, 1925, George Washington Carver received a patent for a pomade, or cream, made from peanuts. Both the product and the process whereby the cosmetic was created were patented. This authorization meant that only Carver could grant permission for a company or an individual to manufacture this particular pomade.

During the Great Depression in the summers of 1930 and 1931 the crops of Mississippi farmers were devastated by a severe drought. As the drought-damaged crops would not produce seeds, the Red Cross distributed them to farmers. These seeds could then be used to cultivate crops the following year. This photograph documents farmers lined up to receive free seeds from Red Cross relief workers.

During the 1930s, a movement called chemurgy began, which sought to develop new products from crops. Naturally, the leaders of this movement turned to Carver for help. One of the leaders was Henry Ford, the wealthy founder of the Ford Motor Company, a maker of automobiles. Ford asked Carver to give the main speech at a chemurgy meeting in Michigan in 1937. Carver's participation in this meeting and other chemurgic conferences gave the movement a great deal of publicity. By that time, however, Carver was in his seventies and

NATURE'S GARDEN FOR VICTORY AND PEACE

Oxalis corniculata—Oxalis
(After Bailey)

tender (preferably in a porcelain or granite ware vessel); rub through a sieve, add your favorite seasoning and three cups of soup stock to it; thicken with one tablespoonful of butter and one of flour rubbed together, and stir this into a teacupful of boiling hot milk. Add to the soup stirring it vigorously to prevent curdling. Let boil up and serve at once with croutons or toasted crackers.

POTATO FAMILY (Solanaceae)

IRISH POTATO, WHITE POTATO, etc. (Solanum tuberosum). The tender shoots and leaves are a fine addition to add to a pot of mixed greens, greatly improving the flavor.

HORSE NETTLE, BULL NETTLE, SANDBRIER, TREAD SALVE, etc. (Solanum Carolinense). The young, tender tops add much to a pot of mixed greens.

MINT FAMILY (Menthaceae)

The following are pot herbs, used in the preparation of foods largely for their flavoring qualities:

PENNYROYAL (Hedeoma pulegioides)

LEMON BALM, GARDEN BALM, SWEET BALM, etc. (Melissa officinalis)

—14—

Carver's 1942 Bulletin #43 *Nature's Garden for Victory and Peace* contained instructions on preparing a number of wild plants for human consumption. Plants in the wood sorrel family, shown above in a drawing by Carver, could be used in pies, salads, and soups.

This 1942 photo of George Washington Carver and Henry Ford documents the meeting of the two friends after Ford donated the funds to install a modern laboratory for food research in Dearborn, Michigan. Because his friend's health was failing, Ford had installed an elevator in Carver's Tuskegee dormitory the previous year.

unable to do much research. Ford and Carver became good friends. Ford built a cottage, which simulated Carver's birthplace, as well as a nutritional laboratory near his home in Dearborn, Michigan, to honor Carver. Ford later paid to have an elevator installed in a Tuskegee building where his old friend lived, when Carver began to have difficulty climbing stairs.

In 1938, Carver declared, "I am not a finisher. I am a blazer of trails. Little of my work is in books. Others must take up the various trails of truth, and carry them on." Carver took two important actions to see that this would happen. He established a museum to display his work and to inspire followers. Carver also gave nearly $60,000 of his life savings to set up the George Washington Carver Foundation at Tuskegee. This institution would provide money and a place for other researchers to continue Carver's work and to further his ideals. Both the museum and the foundation are still in existence at Tuskegee University and are an important part of Carver's legacy.

Carver's ability to accumulate that much money demonstrated that what he preached actually worked. Carver earned less than $50,000 during the forty-seven years he was at Tuskegee. He used little of his earnings, saving both the money and the interest it accumulated in banks. Instead of buying expensive goods, he recycled his and other people's trash. Carver would make rag rugs out of his old clothes, but only after he had worn them as long

The Carver Museum is located on the Tuskegee Institute campus in Macon County, Alabama. Carver hoped his museum would motivate schoolchildren and potential scientists. When they viewed the exhibits on display he thought they might "catch the spirit" behind his life's work.

as possible. His own life demonstrated that people could meet a lot of their needs without spending a cent.

After Carver died on January 5, 1943, many people claimed that he had saved the South from its dependence on cotton. Others called him one of the world's greatest inventors and chemists. His fame continued to grow even after he died. Schools and libraries were named for him, and postage stamps bore his picture.

Some people, however, have questioned Carver's accomplishments. They point out that none of his new uses for peanuts became successful products for sale.

People call Carver the inventor of peanut butter, but it already existed before he became interested in the nut. Carver did not use good scientific methods, such as keeping detailed records of his work. Finally, he was only one of many people who urged the South to grow crops other than cotton.

Most scholars agree that Carver had the ability to be a great scientist. He could have made important contributions in mycology or hybridization at Iowa State. If Carver had stayed there, however, few people would have ever heard of him. Few scientists become famous.

Some people have claimed that Carver achieved fame because he won the approval of white southerners.

In this 1943 photo, two cadets from the Tuskegee Institute watch over George Washington Carver's open casket. Carver was buried in Tuskegee's cemetery.

Carver did not say things that made them angry. He dressed and acted humbly, which pleased those who thought whites were better than blacks. Supporters of slavery and segregation, such as the UDC, said Carver's success proved that neither institution really harmed African Americans who were willing to work hard. They held Carver up as an example of how black children should act. Whites did not want their black neighbors to follow the lead of those who openly stood up for their rights. Such black leaders as William Edward Burghardt Du Bois scared and angered whites. As one of the founders of the NAACP, Du Bois

Professor W.E.B. Du Bois (*standing at right*) was photographed around 1932 at the headquarters of *Crisis*, the NAACP's publication. The journal, which was first published in 1910, sought to end the lynching of African Americans. Du Bois was the editor of *Crisis* until 1934.

constantly fought to end segregation and lynching. W.E.B. Du Bois and others criticized Carver because he didn't say more about the continual mistreatment of African Americans.

The approval of southern whites did help to make Carver famous. On the other hand, not all white people in the South and elsewhere supported segregation. Some individuals sought to convince other whites to respect African Americans. These whites, too, used Carver's life to make their point. Carver became a symbol of black ability. Many black young people were inspired by Carver to become scientists. In fact, Carver became a symbol for many different groups.

Often these groups disagreed with one another, but they all contributed to Carver's fame. A scientist who openly spoke of his faith in God reassured religious people, who believed that too many scientists had made science and technology their new religion. During the Great Depression, Americans became discouraged. Some had lost everything they owned and began to wonder if hard work really did pay off. Carver's success was a symbol of hope for them. The United Peanut Association turned Carver into the Peanut Man to sell more nuts. The chemurgy movement adopted him as well. As Carver was useful to so many causes, some people think those causes exploited Carver for their own purposes. Carver was, however, a friend as well as a symbol to the people who praised him the most.

The Peanut Man was a myth, but the real Carver deserves honor. He helped hundreds of poor farmers to have better lives. He inspired black students and white students to help others. He was a great teacher and a loving friend to many different kinds of people. Carver gave his help free of charge to business owners and others. His success encouraged black children to get an education.

Carver also blazed the trail for those who wish to pro-

Earth Day is an annual event that was first launched in 1970 with the goal of increasing the public's awareness toward the care of our environment. This poster was designed by Yukihisa Isobe in 1970. The arrows symbolize the environmental goals of reducing, reusing, and recycling materials to create less waste and pollution on Earth.

tect the environment. For a long time people did not care what impact their actions had on the world. In the United States everyone believed there was an unlimited supply of land, water, and minerals such as coal and oil. Few Americans tried to conserve these resources. Burning fuels such as coal and gas made the air dirty. The reckless use of land killed off species of animals, birds, fish, and insects. Occasionally, someone like Carver would try to make people see the impact of those actions.

Only decades after his death did people begin studying the relationships between plants, animals, and the environment. This field study is called ecology. Calling themselves ecologists, many individuals have sought to find substitutes for items that have become scarce or that hurt the environment. These ecologists urge people to recycle their trash and to conserve water and energy. Carver would have been proud of their efforts. His vision is as useful today as it was when he was living. Perhaps he was a wizard, after all.

Timeline

1864 or 1865	George Washington Carver is born.
1865	The Civil War ends and slavery is abolished.
1877	Carver moves to Neosho, Missouri.
	Carver attends a school for African American children in Neosho.
	The Reconstruction ends.
1879	Carver witnesses a lynching in Fort Scott, Kansas. The experience is so terrifying that Carver flees town and moves to Olathe, Kansas.
1881	Booker T. Washington founds the Tuskegee Normal and Industrial Institute in Macon County, Alabama.
1885	Carver applies by mail for admission to Highland College and is accepted. When he arrives on campus Carver is turned away from the college because he is African American.
1886	Carver becomes a homesteader in Ness County, Kansas. The Homestead Act of 1862 grants settlers 160 acres (64.8 ha) of land if they remain on the property for five years and pay a fee of $24.
1888–1889	Carver leaves Ness County and supports himself by opening a laundry business in Winterset, Iowa. He befriends the Milhollands, who encourage him to apply to Simpson College in Indianola, Iowa.
1890	Carver enters Simpson College as an art major.
1891	Carver transfers to Iowa State to study agriculture.
1893	Carver's painting *Yucca and Cactus* is exhibited at the

	World's Columbian Exposition in Chicago, Illinois.
1896	Carver gets a master's degree in agriculture from Iowa State and accepts a job at Tuskegee Institute.
	The Supreme Court rules in *Plessy v. Ferguson* that segregation is legal.
	Tuskegee receives money to open an agricultural experiment station.
1897	One of Carver's former professors, James Wilson, becomes the U.S. secretary of agriculture.
1906	The Jesup Wagon starts taking its movable school to farmers.
1915	Booker T. Washington dies.
1916	Carver agrees to serve on the advisory board of the National Agricultural Society.
	Carver is invited to join the British Royal Society of Arts.
	Carver publishes one of his most famous bulletins, *How to Grow the Peanut and 105 Ways of Preparing It for Human Consumption*.
1917	The United States enters World War I, and Carver seeks substitutes for scarce goods.
1920	Carver speaks at the meeting of the United Peanut Association of America.
1921	Carver addresses Congress to win a tariff for peanuts.
1923	Both the United Daughters of the Confederacy and the National Association for the Advancement of Colored People honor Carver.
	Atlanta businessmen found the Carver Products Company to sell Carver's inventions.

1929   The stock market crashes and the Great Depression begins, causing many people to lose their jobs.

Carver begins to return his focus to telling people how to use natural resources to meet their needs.

1930   During a train ride, Carver is forced to move to a segregated railroad car in Oklahoma City, Oklahoma.

1931   Tom Huston commissions a bronze plaque of Carver, which is donated to Tuskegee.

1937   Henry Ford asks Carver to speak at a chemurgy meeting in Michigan.

1940   Carver donates his life savings of almost $60,000 to establish the George Washington Carver Foundation at Tuskegee.

1941   The Carver Museum on the Tuskegee campus is opened to the public.

1943   Carver dies and is buried at Tuskegee.

Glossary

abolitionists (a-buh-LIH-shun-ists) Men and women who worked to end slavery.

alleged (uh-LEJD) Not proven in a court of law.

botany (BAH-tun-ee) The study of plants.

chemurgy (KEM-er-jee) The study of ways to make manufactured items out of crops.

compost (KOM-pohst) A mixture of decaying matter, such as leaves, used as a fertilizer.

Confederacy (kun-FEH-duh-reh-see) The eleven southern states that declared themselves separate from the United States in 1860 and 1861.

credit (KREH-dit) To buy something and promise to pay for it later.

debt (DET) Something owed.

demonstration agents (deh-mun-STRAY-shun AY-jents) People who go out into the community to show farmers better methods of farming.

denominations (dih-nah-meh-NAY-shunz) Groups of churches that share the same beliefs and join together, such as Baptists and Methodists.

devout (dih-VOWT) Very religious.

ecology (ee-KAH-luh-jee) The study of the relationships between living things and their environment.

environment (en-VY-ern-ment) Everything that surrounds human beings and other organisms, and everything that makes it possible for them to live.

exploited (ek-SPLOYT-ed) Used for a selfish reason.

exposition (ek-spuh-ZIH-shun) A public display, similar to a fair, that shows art and industrial advances.

frontier (frun-TEER) The edge of a settled country, where the wilderness begins.

frustrations (frus-TRAY-shunz) Feelings of discouragement when one has difficulty doing something.

homesteader (HOHM-steh-der) A person who settles on land granted by the government under the Homestead Act.

horticulture (HOR-teh-kul-cher) The science of growing plants.

innovations (ih-nuh-VAY-shunz) Creations of new things.

nitrogen (NY-truh-jen) An odorless gas found in minerals and proteins.

nutrition (noo-TRIH-shun) The act of getting the food that living things need to live and to grow.

philanthropist (fih-LAN-thruh-pist) One who practices goodwill toward others; a charitable person.

provisions (pruh-VIH-zhuns) Food and supplies.

Reconstruction (ree-kun-STRUK-shun) The reorganization of the South after the Civil War. Attempts were made to guarantee black voting rights and to see that prominent former Confederates did not dominate local governments.

sanitation (sa-nih-TAY-shun) The disposal of trash and human waste.

segregation (seh-gruh-GAY-shun) The act of keeping people of one race, sex, or social class apart from others.

stereograph (STAYR-ee-oh-graf) A picture taken by a camera that has two lenses, which makes the image appear to be three-dimensional.

Union (YOON-yun) The northern states that stayed loyal to the federal government during the Civil War.

Additional Resources

To learn more about George Washington Carver and Tuskegee, check out these books and Web sites:

Books

Means, Florence Crannell. *Carver's George, a Biography of George Washington Carver*. Boston: Houghton Mifflin, 1952.

Nelson, Marilyn. *Carver, a Life in Poems.* Asheville, N.C.: Front Street Books, 2001.

Wellman, Sam. *George Washington Carver: Inventor and Naturalist.* Urichsville, O.H.: Barbour Publishing, 1998.

Web Sites

Due to the changing nature of Internet links, PowerPlus Books has developed an online list of Web sites related to the subject of this book. This site is updated regularly. Please use this link to access the list:
www.powerkidslinks.com/lalt/gwcarver/

Bibliography

Adair, Gene. *George Washington Carver*. New York: Chelsea House, 1989.

Elliot, Lawrence. *George Washington Carver: The Man Who Overcame*. Englewood Cliffs, N.J.: Prentice-Hall, 1966.

Holt, Rackham. *George Washington Carver, an American Biography*. Garden City, N.Y.: Doubleday, 1963.

Jones, Allen W. "The Role of Tuskegee Institute in the Education of Black Farmers." *Journal of Negro History* 60, no. 2, (1975): pages 252-267.

Kitchens, John W. and Lynne B., eds. *George Washington Carver Papers at Tuskegee [microform]*. Tuskegee Institute, AL: Carver Research Foundation, 1975.

Kremer, Gary R., ed. *George Washington Carver in His Own Words*. Columbia: University of Missouri Press, 1987.

Litwack, Leon F. *Trouble In Mind: Black Southerners in the Age of Jim Crow*. New York: Vintage Books, 1999.

McMurry, Linda O. *George Washington Carver, Scientist and Symbol*. New York: Oxford University Press, 1981.

Ward, Geoffrey C. *The West: An Illustrated History*. Boston: Little, Brown & Company, 1996.

Index

About the Author

Linda McMurry Edwards is an emeritus professor of African American history at North Carolina State University. She is retired from teaching but still works with graduate students. After getting her Ph.D. from Auburn University, she taught for twenty-five years and published three biographies: *George Washington Carver, Scientist and Symbol*; *Recorder of the Black Experience, A Biography of Monroe Nathan Work*; and *To Keep the Waters Troubled, the Life of Ida B. Wells*. Linda is also the coauthor of the college-level textbook, *America and Its Peoples: A Mosaic in the Making*. She plans to continue writing and to enjoy her retirement with her husband, John A. Edwards.

Primary Sources

Cover. George Washington Carver, photo, 1906, Frances Benjamin Johnston, Library of Congress Prints and Photograph Division, Background, Students working in the fields of Tuskegee's experiment station, photo, Culver Pictures. **Page 4**. George Washington Carver, photo, ca. 1915, Hulton/Archive by Getty Images. **Page 8**. Tuskegee Institute, photo, 1881, Bettmann/CORBIS. **Page 10**. Colored Service in Rear, sign, metal and paint, ca. 1900s, Amistad Foundation, Simpson. **Page 13**. Railroad map and guide to Missouri, 1872, Asher & Adams, Library of Congress Geography and Map Division. **Page 14**. Moses Carver, photo, Culver Picture. **Page 22**. Harper's Ferry Insurrection, wood engraving, 1859, CORBIS. **Page 24**. Fort Scott, stereograph, ca. 1870, Tresslar Brothers Studio, Kansas State Historical Society. **Page 25**. The Lexington Laundry, Richmond, Virginia, photo, ca. 1899, Library of Congress Prints and Photographs Division. **Page 26**. Negro Refugees on the Levee, photo, April 17, 1897, Library of Congress Prints and Photographs Division. **Page 28**. Simpson College, photo, July 20, 1907, Frederick J. Bandholtz, Library of Congress Prints and Photographs Division. **Page 31**. Carver at Simpson College art class, photo, 1890, Simpson College Archives, Indianola, Iowa. **Page 32**. Joseph Lancaster Budd, photo, close-up reproduced from the original, Special Collections at the University Libraries of Notre Dame. **Page 33**. Iowa State yearbook photo of Carver, photo, 1894, Iowa State University. **Page 34**. Palace of Mechanic Arts and Lagoon at the World's Columbian Exposition, Chicago, Illinois, photo, 1892, Frances Benjamin Johnston, Library of Congress Prints and Photographs Division. **Page 36**. James Wilson, photo, ca. 1906, Frances Benjamin Johnston, Library of Congress Prints and Photographs Division. **Page 40**. Booker T. Washington, photo, ca. 1900, Library of Congress Prints and Photographs Division. **Page 41**. Faculty of Tuskegee Institute, photo, Library of Congress Prints and Photographs Division. **Page 45**. Verdict on *Plessy v. Ferguson*, U.S. Supreme Court, No.

210, October Term, 1895, U.S. Supreme Court. **Page 47**. Negro homes, Chattanooga, Tenn., photo, 1899, Library of Congress Prints and Photographs Division. **Page 49**. Andrew Carnegie, photo, 1913, Marceau, Library of Congress Prints and Photographs Division. **Page 52**. Chemistry laboratory at Tuskegee Institute, Hulton/Archive by Getty Images. **Page 55**. Tuskegee Institute chapel, photo, ca. 1900, Culver Pictures. **Page 57**. Tuskegee Normal and Industrial Institute, photo, ca. 1916, Haines Photo Co., Library of Congress Prints and Photographs Division. **Page 61**. (*See cover.*) **Page 64**. Bulletin #26. *When, What and How to Can & Preserve Fruits and Vegetables in the Home*, Experimental Station, Tuskegee Normal and Industrial Institute, Tuskegee, Alabama, pamphlet, 1915, Tuskegee. **Page 66**. *George Washington Carver*, photo, 1906, Frances Benjamin Johnston, Library of Congress Prints and Photographs Division. **Page 67**. Agents and rural nurse with movable school, 1923, G. W. Ackerman, NARA. **Page 70**. Cotton plant, photo, ca. 1896, Charles Napier Lochman, Academy of Natural Sciences of Philadelphia/CORBIS. **Page 74**. Bulletin #31. *How to Grow the Peanut and 101 Ways of Preparing it for Human Consumption*, Experiment Station, Tuskegee Normal and Industrial Institute, Tuskegee, Alabama, 1925, pamphlet, Tuskegee. **Page 82**. N.A.A.C.P. Spingarn award medal, front view, 1924, Library of Congress Prints and Photographs Division. **Page 84**. Thomas Alva Edison, photo, ca. 1911, Library of Congress Prints and Photographs Division. **Page 85**. Railroad porter, photo, 1905, Kansas State Historical Society. **Page 89**. U.S. Patent 1,522,176 given to Carver on January 6, 1925, US Patent Office. **Page 90**. Red Cross workers distributing seeds, photo, 1931, Lewis Wickes Hine, Hulton/Archive by Getty Images. **Page 91**. Bulletin #43 *Nature's Garden for Victory and Peace*, Experiment Station, Tuskegee Normal and Industrial Institute, Tuskegee, Alabama, pamphlet, 1942, Tuskegee. **Page 92**. George Washington Carver and Henry Ford, photo, 1942, Bettmann/CORBIS. **Page 95**. George Washington Carver's Open Casket, photo, 1943, Bettmann/CORBIS. **Page 96**. W.E.B. Du Bois and the staff of *Crisis*, photo, ca. 1932, Hulton/Archive by Getty Images.

Credits

Photo Credits

Cover, pp. 25, 26, 28, 34, 36, 40, 41, 47, 49, 57, 66, 82, 84, 94, 98 Library of Congress Prints and Photographs Division; cover (background), pp. 14, 51, 55, 61, Culver Pictures; pp. 4, 52–53, 90, 96 © Hulton/Archive by Getty Images; pp. 8, 92, 95 © Bettmann/CORBIS; p. 10 Courtesy of the Wadsworth Atheneum Museum of Art, Amistad Foundation, Simpson Collection; p. 13 Library of Congress Geography and Map Division; p. 22 © CORBIS; pp. 24, 85 Kansas State Historical Society; p. 31 Courtesy of the Simpson College Archives, Indianola, Iowa; p. 32 Reproduced from the original held by the Department of Special Collections at the University Libraries of Notre Dame; p. 33 Iowa State University; p. 45 U.S. Supreme Court; pp. 64, 74, 91 Courtesy of the Tuskegee National Historic Site and George Washington Carver National Monument; p. 67 Still Picture Branch, National Archives and Records Administration; p. 70 © Academy of Natural Sciences of Philadelphia/CORBIS; p. 72 Courtesy of Donald W. Hyatt; p. 79 © Royal Society; p. 89 U.S. Patent Office.

Project Editor
Daryl Heller

Series Design
Laura Murawski

Layout Design
Corinne L. Jacob

Photo Researcher
Jeffrey Wendt